Built From Scratch

Hire & Lead
A
Remote Team

by

Brian Turner

First Edition
2025

First Edition

ISBN: *979-8-9937162-1-3*

BUILT FROM SCRATCH: Hire & Lead a Remote Team

Table of Contents

Chapter 1: The Rebuild

Every builder hits a point where effort stops working. This was mine.

I didn't set out to build a remote team.
I just wanted control.

Back in 2014, I was trying to build an app with a New York-based company. They outsourced everything overseas. I didn't understand their language or their logic, but I needed their skill. Every call felt like guessing. Every update sounded right until it wasn't.

The app worked. But it wasn't mine.
It was a version of my idea that belonged to someone else.

A second Indian company reached out. They promised to clean up what the first team left behind. The pitch sounded confident, and the price made sense. They rebuilt pieces of the app that worked. The designs were cleaner, the response time was faster, and for a while, I thought I had cracked it.

Then the cracks started to show.
Dead links appeared in the backend. Exposed user data. Code that only one developer understood. Every improvement came with a hidden flaw that would cost twice as much to repair. There was no version control, no documentation, no real system

holding it together. If one person disappeared, the whole thing stalled.

My first lesson in remote work: cheaper isn't freedom. It's just a different kind of risk.
The invoice looked lighter, but I was paying in time, trust, and control.

By 2018, I had had enough of middlemen. I stopped hiring companies and started hiring people.
Real people. Designers who showed their work, developers who explained clearly, assistants who noticed the details I missed. I learned to test on small projects before committing to big ones. I learned to read tone in emails. I learned that communication is culture.

Each new hire became a small experiment in trust. Some worked. Some vanished. Every loss cost less because it taught me what to look for the next time. Every success gave me one more reason to believe I could build quietly, piece by piece.

I was still learning, but curiosity kept me moving forward.

Then 2020 came.

I was living in Miami, running a home care business in Maryland. COVID hit. Payroll spiked. Revenue dropped. Local hires kept missing. I trusted people who said the right things but couldn't deliver. Every mistake was expensive, and every delay cost twice as much.

I kept thinking I could fix it by working harder.
That was the lie that burned the most.

I was sitting in a WeWork one afternoon, looking at the numbers, trying to figure out how long I could hold on. The math didn't work. The structure didn't either.

That's when I remembered what I had learned while building that app.
If people across the world could bring my ideas to life from a laptop, why couldn't they help me rebuild this?

I didn't need a bigger team. I needed a better one.
I didn't need more effort. I needed alignment.

That's when I started rebuilding everything around systems, not presence. Around proof, not promises.

I stopped chasing people who needed managing and started building with people who wanted to build.

Freedom isn't about being everywhere. It's about everything still running when you're not.
That's the foundation of remote.
Not distance.
Discipline.

Chapter 1.1: Freedom vs. Control

I grew up hearing it everywhere: *work on the business, not in the business.*
It sounded simple.
Until I tried to live it.

Working on the business means strategy, systems, and leverage; working in the business means survival.
Most people spend their whole lives surviving and calling it success.

I watched people build things that looked impressive on paper but cost them everything they had built.They made money but could never buy back time. They hired staff, but still had to show up for every problem. It was the illusion of control disguised as ownership.

When I read *The 4-Hour Workweek*, it shattered that illusion. It wasn't about escaping work but redesigning it.
Tim Ferriss taught that freedom comes from systems, not effort. That book planted the seed for everything I've done since: the belief that your business should give you time, not take it.

Most builders get trapped in control.
They mistake control for clarity.
They think approving every decision makes them

leaders. It doesn't. It means fear disguised as control.

Control feels safe. It makes you think you are protecting the business when you are really protecting your comfort zone. But comfort is expensive. It costs creativity, growth, and bandwidth.

Real freedom doesn't come from control.
It comes from clarity.

Clarity about what actually moves the business forward.
Clarity about what you should stop touching.
Clarity about who can own the outcome when you're not around.

The goal of building remote is not to escape work. It is to escape dependence.

When you hold on too tightly, you become the bottleneck.
When you delegate without systems, you create chaos.
Freedom lives between those two extremes.

That space is called alignment.

In *Aligned AF*, I wrote that alignment is what keeps builders from breaking. It's not balance. It's order. It's when your habits, priorities, and people point in the same direction. When that happens, control becomes unnecessary. You do not have to manage what is already aligned.

Alignment in remote teams looks like this: everyone knows the goal, the standard, and the why.
They move without waiting for you. They think ahead. They protect the rhythm.

You can't scale what you don't trust.
And you can't trust what you haven't built.

That's where control dies and leadership begins.

Freedom without structure is a vacation.
Freedom with structure is a business.

You earn that structure one process at a time.
You document. You automate. You delegate.
You teach people to move how you move.

Over time, you start to see it, the less you chase control, the more influence you have.
People rise to the level of trust you give them.
And when they do, you finally have space to build again.

That is what freedom really means for a builder. Not doing nothing, but doing only what matters.
Doing only what matters.

Freedom is not the absence of control. It's the evolution of it.
Control holds.
Freedom builds.

Chapter 1.2: The Time Trap

Every builder who escapes control eventually runs into time.

You stop micromanaging people, but you start micromanaging hours.
You free your calendar, but fill it again with different forms of noise.

The time trap is subtle. It makes you feel productive while quietly stealing the space you built.

We were raised to believe time equals effort and effort equals value.
That logic works when you have a job. It destroys you when you have a vision.

The truth is, builders don't get paid for hours.
We get paid for outcomes.

You cannot measure leadership in time. You measure it in results, trust, and direction.

The trap starts when you mistake motion for progress and stay busy because busy feels useful. You take every call. You answer every message. You tell yourself you are holding things together, but you are really avoiding the one thing that would move everything forward: structure.

Time is a mirror. It reflects what you have designed and what you have not.

If your day runs you, it is because you never taught it how to behave.

Remote leadership exposes this fast. You cannot watch everyone. You cannot 'walk around' to feel productive. You have to build rhythms that replace your presence.

That is how you buy back time, by teaching your systems to tell you the truth.

Trello boards replace status meetings.
Recorded Looms replace repeat explanations.
Weekly scorecards replace daily check-ins.
Clear priorities replace constant pings.

Every tool that saves you time only works if you use it with discipline.
Automation doesn't fix disorder. It multiplies it.

Builders fall into the time trap when they automate chaos.
Freedom is not about doing less. It is about spending time only on what multiplies.

That's where alignment comes in again.

When your goals, people, and processes point in the same direction, you stop managing time, and start designing it. You move from reacting to creating, from calendar-driven to purpose-driven.

The best remote builders don't work more or less than anyone else.
They just work with intention.

They build mornings that anchor them, afternoons that produce, and evenings that reset.
They treat their schedule like architecture, not a checklist.

You do not need more time. You need a better structure for the time you already have.

Because time will continually expand to fit your lack of clarity.

Once you understand that, you stop asking how to manage time and start asking how to protect it.

Protect it from distraction.
Protect it from meetings.
Protect it from people who confuse access with importance.

That's how you break the trap.

You stop measuring your value by how long you worked today and start measuring it by what still works when you don't.

Time doesn't create freedom. Structure does.
Freedom is how you spend it.
Discipline decides if you keep it.

Chapter 1.3: Systems Before Staff

Most people build their business backwards.
They hire before they design.

They tell themselves they need "help," but what they really need is order.

Adding people to a broken system doesn't fix it. It multiplies the mess.

Every builder who's been through it knows, you don't hire to create structure. You create structure so your hires can thrive.

Systems are the language your business speaks when you're not there.

Before you hire anyone, you have to decide how you want things done.
That's not about perfection. It's about consistency.

Document everything once.
The way you send emails. The way you onboard clients. The way you name files. The way you close your day.

If it matters enough to repeat, it matters enough to record.

The first real system you build is a mirror of how you think.

It shows you where you're clear and where you're still guessing.

That's why most founders avoid it. Systems expose the truth. They make you realize you've been running on memory, not process.

But once you start, everything changes.

When you write things down, you stop teaching from frustration.
You start teaching from clarity.

When you build a workflow, you stop reacting.
You start predicting.

When you design systems, you stop asking for accountability and start planning for it.

That's how remote teams win.

They don't rely on supervision. They rely on visibility.

Visibility means everything has a place and a rhythm.
Tasks live in a project board.
Notes live in a shared doc.
Updates live in one channel, not ten.

Once your information is organized, people can actually perform.

This is where tools like Trello, Asana, Notion, and Google Drive come in, but tools aren't the system.

They're the vehicle. The system is how you use them.

A messy Trello board is just a digital version of your desk.

Structure isn't about software. It's about intention.

Start simple.
Create one clear folder for operations.
One for marketing.
One for finance.
Inside each, document the repeatable steps that keep your business alive.

Test your systems before you bring someone into them.
If it doesn't work for you, it won't work for anyone you hire.

Remote leadership isn't about finding the perfect team.
It's about creating a framework where imperfect people can do excellent work.

That starts with you.

Systems create freedom. People sustain it.
Build the structure first.
Then build the team to protect it.

Chapter 1.4: How to Know What to Outsource First

Most builders wait too long to get help.
Then they hire for the wrong reason.

They think outsourcing is about removing what they hate.
It's really about removing what holds them back.

You don't start by asking, 'What do I want off my plate?' You start by asking, 'What keeps me from building?'

Outsourcing is a math problem, not a mood.

If you're spending hours on something that doesn't multiply results, it's time to delegate it.

Freedom doesn't come from handing off work.
It comes from handing off the right work.

---

1. Start With Energy, Not Ego

There are things you can do.
There are things you should do.
And there are things that drain you every time you do them.

The first category is skill.
The second is strength.
The third is noise.

Outsource the noise first.

These are tasks that demand effort but give you no growth.
The reports you redo every week.
The emails you rewrite every day.
The admin details that keep you from moving forward.

If a task drains your energy but doesn't develop your business, it belongs to someone else.

---

2. Know Your Builder Zone

Your Builder Zone is where your skill and impact overlap.

If you're great at writing and it builds revenue, that's your zone.
If you're good at design but it distracts you from building, that's not your zone.

You hire to protect your zone, not expand it.

Stay where your ideas, energy, and income align.
Everything else is leverage.

---

3. Start With Processes You Can Explain

If you can't explain what you want done, you can't outsource it.

The best first hires are the ones who can execute a clear process, something you've already tested and documented.

It's not their job to create your system. It's their job to run it.

So start with the repeatable things:

- Inbox management

- Calendar coordination

- Social media scheduling

- Customer follow-ups

- Data entry and reporting

These are low-risk, high-volume tasks that free up mental space.

The goal isn't perfection. It's proof.
You're testing your systems and your ability to delegate clearly.

4. Outsource to Learn, Not to Escape

Every new hire teaches you something about your business.
Where it's organized. Where it's not.

When you outsource too early, you learn expensive lessons.
When you outsource intentionally, you buy insight.

The right person shows you where your clarity stops.
The wrong person shows you where you ignored it.

Either way, you learn.

---

5. Reinvest the Time You Save

Outsourcing doesn't mean working less. It means working smarter with what's left.

The time you free up is currency.
Spend it on what multiplies: content, systems, strategy, or rest.
All four compound.

If you use that time to scroll, stress, or overthink, the system breaks again.

Outsourcing isn't about delegation.
It's about design.

You're not paying someone to take tasks.
You're paying them to give you bandwidth.

Every hour you buy back should buy you direction.

Freedom grows through leverage.
Leverage starts with clarity.
Clarity begins with knowing what's no longer yours
to do.

Chapter 2: Hiring – Quiet Recruitment

Once your systems are stable, your next challenge is no longer structure.
It is people, the ones who can keep that structure alive.

Most people make hiring loud.
They post job listings, chase candidates, and hope for loyalty.

Quiet builders do it differently.
They attract alignment, not attention.

Hiring is not about finding people.
It is about designing a culture that people can find themselves in.

Remote work made the talent pool global.
It also made the noise louder.
Anyone can apply. Few can actually build.

This chapter is about cutting through that noise.
Not with fancy job descriptions or corporate language, but with clarity, process, and presence.

You are not looking for resumes.
You are looking for rhythm.

The right person does not need to be managed.
They need to be understood.

Quiet hiring is not about saving money. It is about saving time.
It is not about recruiting louder. It is about building clearer.
When you learn how to find the right people quietly, your business learns how to grow loudly on its own.

Chapter 2.1: Finding Talent Without the Noise

The best people rarely apply.
They are already doing the work.

The goal isn't to find people, it's to recognize builders when you see them.

Quiet hiring begins with clarity.
You don't need expensive platforms or paid upgrades.
You need a clear picture of what you want built, and the patience to find someone who works like you do.

---

1. Clarity Before Casting

Most people hire reactively.
Something breaks, someone quits, panic starts.
They post a rushed ad on Indeed and hope a good person shows up.

That is hiring from desperation, not design.

Quiet hiring starts with the opposite.
You define the outcome first.

Ask yourself three simple questions:

1. What exactly do I need done?

2. What type of person thrives doing that?

3. How will I know if they are doing it well?

Once you know those answers, you can find the right person anywhere.
Indeed becomes a tool, not a crutch.

---

2. Focus on Traits, Not Titles

You can teach tasks.
You can't teach temperament.

When you write your job post or send an email, stop listing skills and start describing habits.

Say things like:

> "You find peace in structure."
> "You notice the small things."
> "You finish what you start."

Builders recognize themselves in statements like that.

Hiring quietly means speaking to who someone is, not just what they can do.

---

3. Go Where the Work Already Lives

You do not need LinkedIn Premium to find good people.
You need to be where good work already happens.

Start with what is close:

- **Indeed** for admin, operations, and support roles

- **Upwork** or **OnlineJobs.ph** for project-based specialists

- **Facebook Groups** and **Reddit communities** for creative or niche talent

- **Referrals** from people you trust

The goal isn't to post everywhere.
It's to post where your kind of person already spends time.

Quiet hiring is not about reach.
It's about resonance.

---

4. Test Small Before You Commit Big

Every builder should run what I call a "quiet test."

Give a small, clearly defined project that takes no more than a few hours: a sample spreadsheet, a content draft, or a short research task.

You are not testing perfection.
You are testing response time, detail, and reliability.

How someone handles small work tells you everything about how they will handle big work.

---

5. Build Relationships, Not Just Roles

The best hires often start as short-term help.
If they move with intention, communicate clearly, and deliver, keep them close.

The quiet builder keeps a bench, a list of reliable people who already know their systems.

Next time something breaks, you will not be hiring.
You will be activating.

Quiet hiring is alignment hiring.
You attract what you describe.
You keep what you structure.
And you grow when you find people who care about the work the way you do.

Chapter 2.2: Testing, Not Interviewing

Most interviews are theater.
People rehearse answers, say what they think you want to hear, and leave you guessing, who they really are.

Testing removes the act.
You stop listening for potential and start looking for proof.

---

1. The Quiet Filter

Before you send a test, send one short email.
This step saves hours of interviews and exposes effort before you spend time or money.

Ask three simple questions:

1. What kind of work do you enjoy most, and why?

2. What is your typical schedule or time zone?

3. Tell me about one project you are proud of and what you learned from it.

You are not looking for perfect answers.
You are looking for effort, tone, and awareness.

If someone cannot take five minutes to answer clearly, they will not take ownership later.
Most people will not reply at all.
That silence is your first filter.

The quiet filter is your preview of alignment.
It shows you who reads directions, who writes with care, and who disappears when work gets real.

---

2. The Builder's Rule: Action Reveals Alignment

Quiet hiring replaces conversation with observation. You learn more from a short project than from an hour of questions.

A good test shows you three things:

1. **How they think** – the logic behind their decisions.

2. **How they communicate** – their clarity and consistency.

3. **How they finish** – whether they close loops or leave them open.

You are not testing perfection.
You are testing pattern.

---

3. Design the Test Around Reality

Your test should mirror the real work, not exaggerate it.
If you need an assistant, ask them to organize a sample inbox or summarize a meeting note.
If you need a designer, ask for one layout that follows your brand guide.
If you need a writer, give a short brief and a word count.

Make it real enough to reveal how they work, but short enough to finish within a few hours.
The goal is truth, not pressure.

---

4. Test One Skill and One Behavior

Every test should reveal both competence and character.

Competence proves they can do the task.
Character shows how they handle feedback, time, and clarity.

After sending the test, watch what happens next.
Do they confirm the deadline?
Do they ask smart questions?
Do they deliver early, on time, or with excuses?

The way someone handles a small assignment tells you how they will treat your business.

5. Pay for Every Test

Always pay people for test projects.
It builds respect and filters out those who are chasing free work.

Payment creates commitment. It also sets the tone for future collaboration.

The best builders value fair exchange.
When you pay for the test, you tell people exactly what kind of leader you are.

6. Create a Simple Scoring System

To keep hiring objective, build a quick scorecard. Rate each candidate from one to five in these categories:

- Communication

- Accuracy

- Speed

- Initiative

- Follow-through

You will start to see patterns.
Some people shine in one area and struggle in another.
Hire for reliability first, and brilliance second.

A great attitude can learn a skill.
A skilled person with poor communication cannot learn reliability.

---

7. Debrief and Reflect

After you finish a test round, ask yourself two questions.
Did they make my life easier or harder?
Would I want to work with them again next week?

Your instinct will tell you more than their portfolio.

The test is never only for them.
It also tests your clarity, your process, and your systems.
Every round makes your structure stronger.

Interviews test words.
Projects test truth.

Quiet builders trust patterns, not promises.
They hire people who prove who they are before they ever join the team.

Chapter 2.3: Writing Clear Role Sheets

Most hiring problems start with vague expectations. People fail because the target was never clear.

A role sheet fixes that.
It defines success before the first day begins.

---

1. A Role Sheet Is a Contract of Clarity

A job description sells.
A role sheet aligns.

The goal is not to attract attention but to set direction.

A good role sheet tells a person three things:

1. **Why the role exists**

2. **What outcomes define success**

3. **How they will communicate progress**

When those three are written clearly, you remove confusion before it starts.

---

2. Write the Role, Not the Resume

Avoid long lists of random skills.
Instead, describe what success looks like ninety days in.

Example:

> Within three months, this role will have organized all client folders, automated weekly reports, and created a simple dashboard for tracking leads.

That statement tells the person exactly how to win.

If they do not know what winning looks like, they will create their own version of it, and that is how teams drift.

---

3. Define Ownership, Not Tasks

Tasks are what they do.
Ownership is what they protect.

Instead of listing "send invoices" or "update spreadsheets," write:

> Own all billing and reporting systems so leadership can see real-time data without requesting it.

Ownership creates accountability.
It also gives people permission to lead their lane.

4. Set Clear Communication Rules

Remote teams fail because communication drifts.

Your role sheet should answer three questions:

- How will we communicate? (Slack, email, Trello comments)

- How often will updates happen? (daily, weekly, or by project)

- How do we report blockers or mistakes?

When communication has a rhythm, trust grows naturally.

5. List the Tools and Access

Write down every tool the role needs.
Include links, login info, and file locations.

When someone joins, they should never need to ask, "Where is that?"

Clarity replaces onboarding calls.

6. Include Your Standards

This is where you put the builder stamp on the role.

Examples:

- Respond to all messages within twenty-four hours.

- Document what you build so others can use it.

- Protect the quiet. No unnecessary meetings.

Standards communicate culture.
They show what matters more than metrics.

---

7. Keep It on One Page

A role sheet is not a manual. It is a map.

If it takes more than one page to explain, it is too complicated.
Complexity hides ownership.

One page forces focus.
Focus builds freedom.

Clarity creates confidence.
Confidence builds consistency.
Consistency creates culture.

When you write clear role sheets, you stop managing people and start leading a process. Everyone knows what winning looks like, including you.

Chapter 2.4: Where to Find the Right People

The internet made hiring easier to start and harder to master.
Anyone can post a job.
Few can find the right person.

Good people are everywhere, but alignment is rare.

Quiet hiring is about searching with structure.
You look for patterns, not profiles.

---

1. Start Close Before You Go Wide

Before posting anything online, start with who you already know.
Ask your circle, ask your current team, ask people you have worked with before.

Trust travels through people who already know how you move.

Referrals are the quiet builder's first filter.
When someone stakes their reputation on a recommendation, that candidate usually respects the work.

If you start there, you may never have to post publicly.

2. When You Go Online, Go With Intention

Every platform has its own rhythm.
The key is matching your needs with the right one.

Here are the main platforms that work for remote builders.

Upwork

Best for freelancers and project-based hires.
You can filter by hourly rate, location, and verified reviews.
Start with a small test project, and watch communication more than cost.

OnlineJobs.ph

Great for virtual assistants, admins, and long-term support roles in the Philippines.
Candidates here value consistency and clarity.
Offer fair pay, clear role sheets, and trust. Loyalty grows fast when you lead with respect.

Fiverr Pro

Best for creative or technical one-offs.
Logos, videos, landing pages, podcast edits.
Perfect for small experiments that show who moves fast and clean.

Indeed

Still the strongest for local or hybrid roles.
If your business has a physical presence or local clients, this is where you find reliability.
Be direct in your posting. Write for alignment, not attention.

Facebook Groups and Reddit Communities

Hidden gems.
Look for industry-specific groups where people share real work, not just job ads.
You can find talent by asking questions, not just posting them.

---

3. Always Make It Personal

Quiet hiring is still human.
Technology can help you find people, but connection helps you keep them.

No matter where you find someone, meet them yourself.
Even a ten-minute Zoom call can reveal more than a perfect portfolio.

Look them in the eyes, listen to their tone, and notice their posture, their calm, and how they respond when you pause.

You are not looking for confidence. You are looking for presence.

Body language tells the truth that resumes hide.
Are they engaged, respectful, and curious?
Do they seem grounded or scattered?

When you meet someone face to face, you can feel whether they are building a future or just searching for a gig.

That feeling matters more than a skill list.

---

4. Look for Patterns, Not Portfolios

A clean resume means nothing if the behavior does not match.

In messages, watch how people communicate.
Do they read carefully? Do they follow directions?
Do they ask questions that show understanding?

Builders know that patterns tell the truth.
If someone takes shortcuts in the introduction, they will take shortcuts on your team.

---

5. Pay Attention to Energy

Quiet hiring is emotional intelligence in motion.
Energy shows up in how someone responds.

Fast does not mean frantic.
Slow does not mean lazy.

You can feel when someone takes pride in their work.

That is the energy you hire for.

---

6. Build Your Talent Bench

The best builders keep a small list of people they trust: designers, writers, editors, assistants, coders. Even if you do not need them now, keep their names close.

Your bench becomes your backup.
When something breaks, you can act fast and quietly.

Over time, you will have a group of people who already understand your systems.
You will not have to retrain. You will just re-engage.

**Finding the right people is not about luck.
It is about clarity, rhythm, and consistency.**

You attract what you describe.
You keep what you structure.
You grow when you hire people who care about the work the way you do.

Chapter 3: Leading – Digital Culture

Once you find the right people, the real work begins.
Leadership starts where hiring ends.

Building a remote team is not about managing tasks, it is about designing culture.

Culture is the invisible system that shapes behavior when no one is watching.
In a digital world, culture is not an office; it is a rhythm.
It shows up in how you communicate, how you respond, and how you handle pressure.

Most leaders try to manage by proximity.
They think leadership means being seen, checking in, or staying busy.
But remote leadership is built on trust, not presence.

Your team will not follow your instructions.
They will follow your energy, your structure, and your calm.

Leading remotely means learning to lead quietly.
It means replacing attention with intention.

When you design systems that protect focus, communication, and accountability, you create

digital culture.
Not the kind that needs a slogan, but the kind people feel.

That is the goal of this next chapter: to help you build a team that runs on trust, structure, and quiet confidence.

Chapter 3.1: Setting Expectations in the First Seven Days

The first week sets the rhythm for everything that follows.
If you build it with structure, people rise to it, and if you build it with silence, confusion fills the space.

Leadership is not about control.
It is about clarity, communication, and calm.

Remote teams do not need constant attention.
They need confident direction.

---

1. Start With Vision, Not Rules

When someone joins your team, they are entering your ecosystem.
The first thing they need to understand is *why the work matters*.

Start your first conversation by explaining three things:

1. The mission: what this business is building and why.

2. The standard: how you define great work.

3. The expectation: what progress looks like each week.

Vision creates buy-in.
Rules create fear.
Start with vision, and the rules will make sense later.

---

2. Hold a Face-to-Face Kickoff

Even in remote work, trust starts eye to eye.

Schedule one live call.
Turn your camera on.
Let them see who they are building with.

Use that call to read energy and presence.
Are they engaged, focused, and curious?
Do they take notes?
Do they ask the right questions?

Ask them about their past work experience.
Ask what type of leadership helps them do their best work.
Ask what accountability means to them.
Then listen.

Their answers tell you how to lead them.

The goal of that first call is not instruction.
It is connection.

---

3. Clarify the Rhythm of Communication

Remote teams fail when communication drifts. In the first week, explain your system for staying connected.

Tell them when updates happen, how feedback works, and how to raise a concern.

Example:

- Daily check-ins through Slack or Trello comments

- Weekly progress summaries every Friday

- Immediate communication for issues or blockers

Rhythm builds confidence.
People move better when they know when and how to be heard.

---

4. Walk Through the Role Sheet Together

Go over the role sheet line by line.
This is not just orientation. It is ownership.

Ask them to repeat back how they understand each part.
Listen for where they are unsure.

Clarify what success looks like in their first thirty days.

When expectations are mutual, accountability becomes natural.

---

5. Model the Culture You Want

The first week is not about checking their performance.
It is about showing them how leadership feels here.

Be responsive.
Be clear.
Be calm when things go wrong.

Culture is not what you write. It is what you repeat.

---

6. Give a Small Win Early

Assign one project that matters but is not overwhelming.

The goal is to build momentum.
A small win creates confidence and rhythm.

Follow up personally when they finish.
Acknowledge the effort, not just the result.

Confidence is the fuel that keeps quiet teams moving.

7. Review and Reflect

At the end of the first week, schedule a short check-in.
Ask three simple questions:

1. What went well this week?

2. What could we improve next week?

3. What do you need from me to do your best work?

This is not a performance review.
It is alignment maintenance.

You are teaching them how to communicate like a builder.

The first seven days decide the next seven months.
When you lead with clarity, people rise without being pushed.
When you build trust early, you can lead quietly later.

Chapter 3.2: Building a Culture of Accountability Without Supervision

Accountability is not control.
It is clarity in motion.

Most leaders confuse supervision with leadership.
They believe presence equals performance.
That illusion breaks fast when you go remote.

You cannot watch everyone anymore, you can only design systems that make ownership visible.

---

1. Replace Supervision With Structure

Accountability should not depend on your mood or memory.
It should live inside your systems.

The best teams do not need reminders.
They have routines.

Start with simple visibility tools:

- A shared task board that shows what everyone is working on.

- Weekly reports that summarize outcomes, not hours.

- Regular check-ins that focus on roadblocks, not blame.

Structure is the new supervision.
When the process works, people hold themselves accountable.

---

2. Define Ownership Clearly

Accountability breaks down when no one knows who owns what.

For every project or system, name one owner.
That person does not have to do everything, but they are responsible for the outcome.

Ownership gives people purpose.
It also gives you peace.

When people know their lane, they can take pride in keeping it clean.

---

3. Create Transparent Scoreboards

People move better when they can see progress.
Visibility turns goals into shared responsibility.

A simple spreadsheet or dashboard can change everything.
List the key metrics for your business: sales closed, clients served, tasks completed, content published.

Update it weekly.
Share it with the whole team.

Numbers do not replace conversation, but they keep it honest.
You cannot argue with what everyone can see.

---

4. Build Accountability Into Meetings

If you have meetings, make them short and structured.
Every meeting should answer three questions:

1.   What did we accomplish last week?

2.   What are the top priorities this week?

3.   What support do you need?

Avoid long updates.
Focus on commitments.
Everyone should leave knowing what they owe, and when it is due.

That is how you create a culture of rhythm instead of reminders.

5. Lead With Calm, Not Fear

Accountability fails when fear enters the room.

People stop communicating honestly when they are afraid of being blamed.
Quiet leaders build confidence through consistency.

When something goes wrong, ask questions before you give direction.
What happened?
What did we learn?
What needs to change so it does not happen again?

Blame shuts people down.
Curiosity pulls them forward.

---

6. Reward Ownership, Not Obedience

Micromanagement creates followers.
Clarity creates leaders.

When someone takes initiative, acknowledge it.
When they solve a problem without waiting, celebrate it.

The more you reward ownership, the less you have to enforce accountability.

Over time, people will start managing themselves.

That is the goal.

---

7. Protect the Quiet

Accountability thrives in calm systems.
If everything is urgent, nothing is important.

Protect your team from unnecessary noise: too
many meetings, random messages, or unclear
requests.

Quiet is not absence.
It is space for people to think, create, and perform.

The quieter your leadership becomes, the louder
your results will sound.

**You do not have to watch people to lead them.
You only have to make the work visible, the
standards clear, and the rhythm consistent.**

That is how accountability becomes culture.

Chapter 3.3: Communicating Without Chaos

Communication is either your greatest asset or your biggest leak.
It builds trust or burns time.

Most teams do not fail from lack of talent, they fail from communication that drains instead of directs.

The goal is not to talk more.
It is to say what matters, when it matters, in a way that moves things forward.

---

1. Create a Communication Map

Before you fix communication, you must define it.

A communication map shows what gets said, where, and how often.

Decide what belongs in each space:

- **Email:** formal updates, contracts, client communication.

- **Slack or Chat:** quick questions, daily touch points.

- **Project Tools (Trello, Asana, Notion):** task updates and file sharing.

- **Video Calls:** strategy, training, or problem-solving sessions.

When people know which channel to use, noise decreases and focus returns.

Confusion starts when everything lives everywhere.

---

2. Reduce Meetings, Increase Meaning

Most meetings exist to fix what better structure could have prevented.

Ask yourself before every meeting:
Does this need conversation, or can it be written?

If it can be written, document it.
If it needs to be discussed, set a clear goal and end time.

Meetings should have a single outcome: alignment.
If it does not align, it does not belong.

Keep meetings short.
Record them if possible.
Summarize decisions in writing immediately after.

Documentation keeps the conversation useful long after it ends.

3. Communicate Predictably

Random communication creates anxiety.
Predictable communication builds peace.

Set rhythms for updates, for example:

- Daily check-ins through chat at a set time.

- Weekly summary reports every Friday.

- Monthly one-on-ones for growth and feedback.

When communication has rhythm, trust replaces tension.

4. Write With Clarity, Not Volume

Good writing is a leadership skill.
It saves time, prevents confusion, and earns trust.

When writing updates or instructions, use short sentences and direct language.
State the goal, the next step, and the deadline.

Example:

Please review the attached design. Leave comments in Trello by Thursday at noon.

That one clear message replaces five follow-ups.

The quieter your messages become, the louder your leadership sounds.

---

5. Protect the Quiet Hours

Constant notifications destroy deep work.

As a leader, model focus.
Turn off alerts for part of the day.
Encourage your team to do the same.

Let people know it is okay to respond, within a reasonable window.
Urgency should be rare, not routine.

You hired people for their skill, not their speed of reply.

Quiet teams move faster because they move with intention.

---

6. Use Technology With Intention

Tools do not create clarity.
They only amplify what already exists.

Choose tools that fit your rhythm, not the other way around.

If a tool feels heavy, simplify it.
If it creates noise, remove it.

The best communication systems are invisible.
They serve the work instead of distracting from it.

---

7. Listen More Than You Announce

Communication is not about broadcasting.
It is about awareness.

Ask your team what works and what feels heavy.
Adjust based on feedback.

You will learn that the best communication rhythm
is the one everyone can sustain.

When you listen first, you communicate leadership
without speaking at all.

Clarity is the highest form of communication.
Noise is the lowest form of leadership.

When your systems speak clearly, you do not have
to.

Chapter 3.4: Building Trust from a Distance

Trust is the foundation of every strong team.
Without it, systems fail quietly and people drift.

In a traditional office, trust is built by proximity.
You see people, greet them, share moments.
Remote work removes that, and what replaces
proximity is consistency.

When people cannot see you, they feel you through
your patterns.

---

1. Be Predictable in Your Leadership

Unpredictable leaders create anxious teams.
The way you show up sets the tone for everyone
else.

Keep your commitments.
Reply when you say you will.
Follow the same process you expect from them.

Predictability is respect; it tells people they can
depend on you even when things get difficult.

---

2. Show Up for People, Not Just Projects

Trust is built in how you respond to people, not just what you assign.

Check in on progress, but also check in on people.
Ask how things are going, not only what is getting done.
When someone struggles, help them realign before you replace them.

Empathy is the quiet form of leadership most people overlook.
It costs nothing and changes everything.

---

3. Communicate Transparently

Secrets destroy trust.
So does silence.

Keep your team informed about goals, challenges, and direction.
You do not have to share every detail, but you should share enough to build inclusion.

When people understand the 'why,' they give more to the 'what.'

Transparency does not mean weakness.
It means maturity.

---

4. Give Feedback the Right Way

Feedback builds trust when it is direct and respectful.

Be specific.
Avoid emotional reactions.
Focus on what happened and what can improve.

Example:

> "The report was late because communication broke down. Let's review the process and fix the timing for next week."

That tone builds accountability without blame.

People trust leaders who tell the truth without making them feel small.

---

5. Share Credit and Take Responsibility

When the team wins, celebrate them publicly.
When mistakes happen, take responsibility privately.

That pattern earns loyalty faster than any bonus.

Leadership is not about being right; it is about keeping the culture right.

---

6. Keep One Channel for Personal Connection

Even in remote work, relationships matter.
Create one space where people can be human.

It could be a casual Slack channel, a group chat, or a short Friday call.
There is no agenda, just connection.

Shared humanity builds trust faster than shared metrics.

---

7. Lead With Grace, Not Guilt

People will make mistakes.
You will too.

What matters is how you recover.

When someone owns a mistake, let them fix it.
Do not turn errors into emotional debt.
Growth happens in a culture of grace, not fear.

Trust grows when people know their mistakes will become lessons, not labels.

Trust is not built by presence; it is built by pattern.
Be consistent.
Be clear.
Be calm.

When your team trusts you from a distance, you have earned real leadership.

Chapter 4: Scaling – Systems That Run Without You

Freedom begins when you stop being the system.
Scaling begins when the system replaces you.

Most builders never reach this stage.
They hire people, build processes, and create structure, but still find themselves buried in the middle.
They become the center of everything they built.

That is not freedom; that is a better-looking cage.

Scaling is not about adding more; it is about removing what keeps you essential.

When your systems can deliver the same result without you watching, you have built real independence.

The goal is not to disappear.
It is to design a machine that moves with or without your hands on it.

Scaling quietly means learning to see your business as architecture.
Each part should have purpose, flow, and resilience.

If you step away for a week, it should hum, and if you step away for a month, it should still breathe.

That level of autonomy does not happen by accident.
It happens through discipline.

This chapter is about building systems that duplicate your best habits and eliminate your worst ones.
It is about turning your structure into momentum.

You already have the people, now it is time to build the machine.

Chapter 4.1: Automate the Repetitive, Not the Human

Automation is not about replacing people.
It is about respecting their time.

You cannot scale chaos; you can only automate clarity.

Most leaders try to automate everything and end up with systems that feel cold and lifeless.
The best builders know what to automate and what to keep human.

Automation should multiply rhythm, not remove relationship.

---

1. Identify the Repetitive Work

The first step in scaling is observation.
Watch your week.
Write down everything that repeats: the messages, the reports, and the tasks that drain focus.

Ask yourself three questions:

1. Does this need creativity or consistency?

2. Does it move the business forward or maintain it?

3. Can it be done the same way every time?

If the answer to all three is yes, automate it.

Automation is not about control. It is about consistency.

---

2. Automate for Accuracy, Not Ego

Do not automate because it looks impressive. Automate because it reduces error.

The right automations do not replace people. They protect them from burnout.

Examples:

- Scheduling software that replaces back-and-forth emails.

- Automatic invoice reminders that prevent missed payments.

- Template-based onboarding systems that keep new hires aligned.

Automation should handle repetition so people can handle refinement.

---

3. Keep Communication Human

The fastest way to lose culture is to automate your voice.

Use automation for structure, not sentiment.
A system can send reminders.
Only a leader can send care.

Examples:

- Use chatbots to confirm information, not deliver feedback.

- Automate reports, but review them with your team.

- Send personal voice notes or quick videos to celebrate wins.

Efficiency should never cost empathy.

---

4. Document Everything Before You Automate

Automation without documentation multiplies confusion.
If you do not understand how a process works manually, do not try to automate it.

Write the steps.
Test them yourself.

Then build automation that mirrors the process exactly.

If something breaks, you can trace it, and if something succeeds, you can replicate it.

Documentation turns automation from magic into management.

---

5. Use Technology as a Teammate

Treat your tools like quiet workers.

Google Workspace, Trello, Zapier, Notion, Airtable, and Slack are all assistants if you train them correctly.
Each one can save hours a week if you use it with purpose.

The key is intention.
Every tool you add should save time, simplify decisions, or make work visible.
If it does not, remove it.

Your tools should feel invisible; if you are constantly managing the system, the system is not helping you.

---

6. Keep Human Touchpoints in the Loop

Automation should open space for connection, not replace it.

Keep moments that remind people, this is still human work:

- Monthly team check-ins.

- Personal thank-you messages.

- End-of-project debriefs where you ask what worked and what can improve.

Technology scales process.
Trust scales people.

---

7. Review and Refine

Automation is not a one-time setup.
It is a rhythm of review.

Once a month, ask yourself:

- What feels heavy?
- What keeps breaking?
- What still depends on me?

Then adjust.

Scaling quietly means your systems evolve while your team keeps moving.

Automate the repetitive and elevate the human. That is how freedom scales without losing soul.

Chapter 4.2: Building Dashboards That Tell the Truth

You cannot manage what you cannot see.
Most leaders make decisions from memory or emotion; that is not strategy, that is survival.

Dashboards remove the guesswork.
They turn emotion into evidence.

A good dashboard does not need to impress.
It needs to inform.

When you can see what matters clearly, you stop reacting and start refining.

---

1. Clarity Before Complexity

Dashboards fail when they are built for aesthetics instead of insight.

Before you open a spreadsheet or platform, ask:
What numbers tell me if the business is healthy?

Start with three core categories:

1. **Performance** – revenue, leads, conversion rates.

2. **Operations** – response time, project completion, client retention.

3. **Team** – tasks finished, communication rhythm, workload balance.

If a number does not change behavior, it does not belong.

Dashboards should show direction, not decoration.

---

2. Choose Simple Tools

You do not need a complex analytics suite to know the truth.

Use what you already have:

- **Google Sheets** for tracking key numbers.

- **Notion or Airtable** for visual dashboards.

- **Trello** or **Asana** for task progress.

- **Zapier**, or **Make (Integromat)**, for automation between tools.

A simple dashboard that updates automatically is better than a beautiful one that requires maintenance.

The goal is to glance, not guess.

---

3. Design for Behavior, Not Vanity

Vanity metrics make you feel good.
Behavioral metrics make you act better.

Ask yourself:
What should this number make me do?

For example:
If leads drop, follow up with marketing.
If client retention falls, review communication habits.
If unfinished tasks increase, adjust scope or staffing.

Dashboards are only valuable if they lead to movement.

---

4. Share the Data Openly

Transparency builds accountability.

Give your team access to the metrics that matter.
Let everyone see the progress in real time.

When people can see how their work contributes to the larger picture, ownership grows naturally.

Numbers replace reminders.
Visibility replaces supervision.

5. Review Weekly, Reflect Monthly

Set a rhythm for review.

Every week, look for trends: what improved, what slipped, what needs attention.
Every month, go deeper: What caused the change, and how can we prevent it next time?

This keeps your leadership proactive instead of reactive.

When data becomes part of the rhythm, you lead from awareness, not surprise.

---

6. Keep One Dashboard for You

Not every metric belongs to the team.
Create one private dashboard for leadership-only numbers: cash flow, debt, profit margins, or personal productivity.

This keeps your focus grounded.

Your leadership dashboard should answer one question:
Can I step away for a week and still know how things are going?

If yes, your systems are working.

7. Let the Numbers Speak

Dashboards tell the truth without emotion.
They show what happened, not what you hoped.

When the data looks good, celebrate.
When it does not, adjust.

Do not argue with what you see; listen to it.
That is the language of scale.

Dashboards are not control, they are clarity.
Clarity lets you lead quietly.
When your systems speak truth, your business
never goes silent.

Chapter 4.3: Delegating Like a Designer

Most people delegate like they are drowning.
They throw tasks at others just to breathe.
That is not leadership; that is panic.

Real delegation feels calm.
It is not about removing work.
It is about redesigning it.

Quiet builders delegate like designers.
They think in systems, not tasks, and they hand off outcomes, not chores.

---

1. Design the Result Before You Delegate the Work

Before you delegate, get clear on what 'done' looks like.

If you cannot describe the outcome, you cannot expect excellence.

Ask yourself:

- What is the goal?

- How will we measure success?

- What does a finished version look like?

Write it down and show examples.
Clarity now prevents confusion later.

Delegation without design creates frustration for both sides.

---

2. Assign Ownership, Not Just Responsibility

Responsibility says, "Do this."
Ownership says, "Protect this."

When people own something, they do more than complete it; they care for it.

Say it clearly:

> "You own client onboarding."
> "You own weekly reporting."
> "You own the website content."

Ownership creates pride.
It also builds leaders instead of followers.

---

3. Match Skill to Scope

Not everyone is ready for every level of ownership.

Match delegation to ability:

- **Beginner:** give clear, repeatable tasks.

- **Intermediate:** give projects with guidelines.

- **Advanced:** give goals and trust their process.

Delegation fails, when you mismatch scope to skill.
Grow people gradually.
As they earn trust, expand their ownership.

---

4. Use the "Explain, Expect, Empower" Framework

This three-step system keeps delegation simple and scalable.

Explain the outcome and context.
Why it matters, who it affects, and what success means.

Expect clarity.
Confirm they understand the assignment and timeline. Ask them to repeat it back.

Empower execution.
Give them the tools, access, and authority to finish without waiting for you.

This turns delegation into duplication.

---

5. Set Checkpoints, Not Chains

Micromanagement kills initiative.
But total silence kills accountability.

Create checkpoints at logical milestones.
Example:

- Day 1: confirm direction.

- Midway: review progress.

- End: final check and feedback.

Checkpoints protect quality, without smothering autonomy.
When the rhythm is predictable, both sides relax.

---

6. Document and Debrief

After a project ends, document what worked and what did not.
Use that insight to refine the next handoff.

Ask three simple questions:

1. What could have been clearer?

2. What slowed us down?

3. What worked well that we can repeat?

Delegation is a skill you sharpen through reflection; the more you learn, the less you repeat.

---

7. Trust the Process You Built

Delegation is not about letting go.
It is about leaning on the systems you created.

If you documented clearly, set checkpoints, and communicated expectations, trust your process.

If someone struggles, fix the system before you fix the person.

Quiet leadership is confidence in your own structure.

Design the work.
Delegate the ownership.
Protect the quiet.

That is how builders multiply results without multiplying chaos.

Chapter 4.4: Knowing When to Step Back

Most builders struggle with one last habit.
They never stop building.

Even after they create systems and hire people, they keep touching everything.
They call it leadership, but it is really fear of stillness.

Stepping back is not absence; it is mastery.

It means trusting the structure you created enough to let it prove itself.

---

1. The Hardest Skill Is Letting Things Run

Freedom feels uncomfortable at first.
You have lived in reaction mode for so long, that calm feels unnatural.

When things run smoothly without you, your instinct is to interfere.
You check in too often, make small changes, or take back control.

That is not leadership; that is habit.

The quiet builder learns to observe instead of intervene.

Your systems cannot grow stronger if you never let them carry the weight.

---

2. Watch the Rhythm, Not the Noise

When you step back, focus on patterns, not moments.

A missed deadline does not mean disaster.
A single problem does not mean failure.

Look for rhythm.
Are tasks still closing?
Are clients still satisfied?
Is the team still communicating?

If the rhythm holds, the system is healthy.

You lead by pattern, not panic.

---

3. Step In Only With Purpose

There will be moments when leadership needs to be visible again.
When standards slip, morale dips, or clarity fades.

That is when you step in not to control, but to recalibrate.

Remind the team of the mission.
Realign the structure.
Then step back again.

Leadership should feel like gravity: steady, constant, invisible until needed.

---

4. Build Self-Correcting Systems

The best systems do not just work.
They adapt.

Teach your team how to identify problems and fix them before they reach you.
Give them permission to improve the process, not just follow it.

A self-correcting system multiplies leadership.
You stop being the decision-maker and become the designer of decisions.

---

5. Protect Your Builder Time

Once your team and systems can run on their own, use that space intentionally.

Do not fill it with new chaos.
Use it to create, to think, and to design the next layer of your business..

Freedom without focus turns into distraction.
Use your reclaimed time to move the vision forward.

That is what separates a builder from a manager.

---

6. Trust the People You Built With

If you hired carefully, trained clearly, and led with
consistency, you can trust your team.
They will make mistakes, but they will also learn.

Trust grows when you stop rescuing everyone.

Give people room to grow through experience.
That is how your culture stays strong even when you
are not around.

---

7. Redefine What It Means to Lead

Leadership is not presence.
It is pattern.

You have built systems that protect time, culture,
and accountability.
Now your job is to keep the rhythm steady.

When you can step back without fear, you know you
have scaled correctly.

That is not the end of building; it is the beginning of
freedom.

You built this to run.
Now let it.

When the work keeps moving without you, that is
not loss of control.
That is proof of design.

Conclusion: The Builder's Manifesto

Freedom was never the goal; it was the test.

Could you build something that works without you?
Could you lead without noise?
Could you trust what you built enough to let it grow?

That is what this journey was really about.

Not working less.
Working right.

Every system, every hire, and every rhythm was a step toward alignment.
Toward peace that does not require presence.

I started developing this mindset many moons ago, when I first read *The 4-Hour Workweek*.
It was the first time I saw work and freedom in the same sentence.
The seed was planted then, but it did not bloom until years later.

I put the vision in motion inside a small WeWork in Miami: just me, a laptop, a few Trello boards, and the belief that there had to be a better way to build.
Then, the travesty of COVID cracked everything open.

It forced me to apply what I had learned to every corner of my business life.

The lesson was quiet, but clear: structure can survive storms.
When the world shut down, systems kept breathing.

That was when I stopped chasing control and started designing freedom.

To everyone who built quietly beside me, thank you. Your consistency made the dream real.

The systems may run without me now, but the mission continues to help others build theirs.

The Builder's Manifesto

1. Build quietly. Let the proof speak.

2. Trust the process you designed.

3. Protect the quiet; it's your greatest advantage.

4. Lead through rhythm, not reaction.

5. Hire for energy, not ego.

6. Design for clarity, not control.

7. Automate the repetitive.

8. Elevate the human.

9. Step back, not away.

10. Always build from alignment.

You built this from scratch, now it builds you.

That is the power of quiet leadership.
That is the rhythm of remote freedom.
That is what it means to lead without being seen.

www.ingramcontent.com/pod-product-compliance
Lightning Source LLC
Chambersburg PA
CBHW071608200326
41519CB00021BB/6918